Dear Parent:

Congratulations! Your child is taking the first steps on an exciting journey. The destination? Independent reading!

STEP INTO READING® will help your child get there. The program offers books at five levels that accompany children from their first attempts at reading to reading success. Each step includes fun stories, fiction and nonfiction, and colorful art. There are also Step into Reading Sticker Books, Step into Reading Math Readers, and Step into Reading Phonics Readers— a complete literacy program with something to interest every child.

Learning to Read, Step by Step!

Ready to Read Preschool–Kindergarten
• big type and easy words • rhyme and rhythm • picture clues
For children who know the alphabet and are eager to begin reading.

Reading with Help Preschool–Grade 1
• basic vocabulary • short sentences • simple stories
For children who recognize familiar words and sound out new words with help.

Reading on Your Own Grades 1–3
• engaging characters • easy-to-follow plots • popular topics
For children who are ready to read on their own.

Reading Paragraphs Grades 2–3
• challenging vocabulary • short paragraphs • exciting stories
For newly independent readers who read simple sentences with confidence.

Ready for Chapters Grades 2–4
• chapters • longer paragraphs • full-color art
For children who want to take the plunge into chapter books but still like colorful pictures.

STEP INTO READING® is designed to give every child a successful reading experience. The grade levels are only guides. Children can progress through the steps at their own speed, developing confidence in their reading, no matter what their grade.

Remember, a lifetime love of reading starts with a single step!

To Alec, Jared, and Vanessa
—E.N.
For Rose, my love and inspiration
—T.L.

Special thanks to Dr. David Grimaldi, Curator, Department of
Entomology at the American Museum of Natural History.

www.stepintoreading.com

Educators and librarians, for a variety of teaching tools, visit us at
www.randomhouse.com/teachers

Library of Congress Cataloging-in-Publication Data
Neye, Emily.
Honeybees / by Emily Neye ; illustrated by Tom Leonard. p. cm. — (Step into reading. A step 2 book)
SUMMARY: Introduces the behavior, habitat, and life cycle of honeybees.
ISBN 0-307-26217-0 (trade) — ISBN 0-307-46217-X (lib. bdg.)
1. Honeybee—Juvenile literature. [1. Honeybee. 2. Bees.]
I. Leonard, Thomas, 1955– , ill. II. Title. III. Series: Step into reading. Step 2 book.
QL568.A6N49 2003 595.79'9—dc21 2002012977

Printed in the United States of America 12 11 10 9 8 7 6 5
First Random House Edition

Honeybees

by Emily Neye
illustrated by Tom Leonard

Random House New York

It's springtime.
A honeybee zips
from bloom to bloom.

We see pretty flowers,
but she sees dinner!

The bee is looking
for nectar and pollen.

Nectar is a sweet juice.
The bee uses her
tongue like a straw
to suck up the nectar.

Pollen is a powder.
The bee pushes the pollen
into hairy baskets
on her back legs.
Then she takes
the food back home.

Honeybees live in hives.
The inside of an old tree
is a good spot for one.

Bees build hives
out of wax.
The wax comes
from their bodies.
They shape it into
small tubes called cells.

Thousands of bees
live in one hive.
The bees work together
like a big team.
The team has one leader.
She is the queen bee.

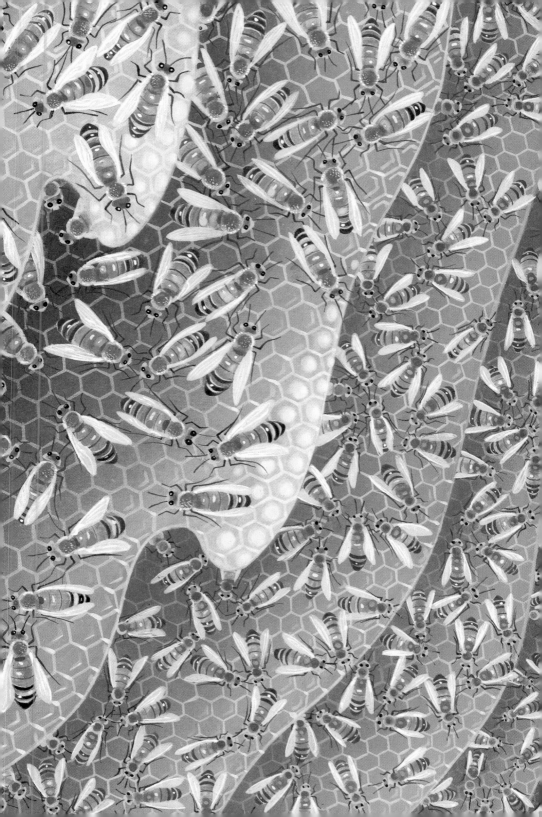

The queen is easy to pick out.
She is bigger than
the other bees.
She is also the only bee
that can lay eggs.

This queen is laying
a tiny egg in the cell.

In a few days,
the egg hatches.
The baby is called a larva.
It looks like a little worm.

But not for long!
Grown bees feed her.
She grows fast.

Soon, the larva stops eating.
The bees seal her cell
with wax.
She is ready for a big change.

Slowly, she grows wings
and legs.
Then she chews away
the wax seal.
Now she is a grown bee!

The grown bee leaves
the hive to look for food.
She finds it in a field
of flowers.
But there is more than
she can carry.
So she goes back to the hive
to "talk" to the other bees.

Bees do not use words
like we do.
They talk by dancing.
They walk, wiggle, and shake.
The dance tells the other bees
where to find the flowers.

Back at the hive,
the bees eat the pollen.
The nectar is put in cells.
The bees mix in chemicals
from their bodies.

They fan the cells
with their wings.
Soon, the nectar
becomes honey.
The bees eat some now.
They save the rest for winter.

Honey is a treat for bees—
and for other animals, too!
This bear tried to steal some
from the hive.
But the bees are fighting back!

A honeybee can sting only once.
Its stinger gets stuck
in the victim's skin.
When the honeybee flies away,
the stinger is pulled
from its body.
The honeybee dies soon after.

A beekeeper's special clothes
protect her from stings.

Beekeepers build hives
for the bees.
They take out honey
and wax to sell.
But they leave behind
plenty for the honeybees.

Winter has come.
There are no more flowers
to visit.
It's a good thing the bees
saved their honey.
It must last all winter.
They huddle and shiver
in the hive to keep warm.

These honeybees have
worked hard.
Now they will rest
and wait for spring.